"Well-defined guardrails to keep your church on the road of disciple making."

—*Jim Putman, author and pastor*

"A great resource for practical ways to make disciples in your church."

—*Dr. Bobby Harrington, author and pastor; director, Discipleship.org*

"I'm personally grateful to God for bringing Brandon and his family to Houston. He's a church planter and practitioner. I've seen how the practices in this book are being worked out at Real Life and in church plants around the city as he's helping train planters in starting disciple making churches. *Stay the Course* is a great read for church planters and will provide guardrails for any church as they instill DNA and remain focused on making disciples."

—*Chad Clarkson, executive director, Houston Church Planting Network*

"*Stay the Course* has been instrumental for our elders and staff team to keep our focus on discipleship. With the help of this resource, we are constantly gaining ground as a disciple making church."

—*Joel Owen, lead pastor, Grace Fellowship Church*

STAY

the

COURSE

*Seven Essential Practices for
Disciple Making Churches*

BRANDON GUINDON

Foreword by **JIM PUTMAN**

To my entire team at Real Life Texas.
Thank you for your commitment to live
out Jesus' call and for staying the course.

CONTENTS

FOREWORD

I am excited about this book by Brandon Guindon. Several years ago, Brandon and the rest of our team came to the conclusion that we needed a very specific process to follow that would make sure we stayed on the road to being a disciple making church. We found that it was easy to have the right ideas, but drift in our application to those ideas. So we went to Scripture and outlined together what concepts we could constantly measure in our church that would ensure ideas led to action. We knew that only as we remained in Christ would we have the heart and power to do ministry, so abiding in Christ had to be first. Then we walked through our understanding of the "Share, Connect, Ministry, and Disciple" process that Jesus modeled. In other words, Jesus *shared* who he was, and then, for those who accepted him, he *connected* with them in relationship, where he taught them the truth. From there, he began to train his disciples for *ministry*, and finally, sent them out to reproduce what they had seen him do with them (*disciple*).

So the guardrails ask these questions of every staff member and ministry in our church: Are we reaching the lost? Are we connecting those who say "yes" to Jesus in relational environments for discipleship? Are there any who have been connected in the past that are beginning to stray? Are we noticing and chasing them? Are we helping people mature in their spiritual growth? How? Are we identifying those with leadership giftings, helping them develop, and releasing them to reproduce what has been done with them? Finally, are we working as a united team and as a church body? Are we aligned? Jesus made it clear that a house divided can't stand.

The guardrails that Brandon Guindon shares in this book keep us straight and force us to answer tough questions as we plan and implement those plans. They give us the ability to measure our success and celebrate when we win. They help us make adjustments when we get off course.

Foreword

Brandon has been one of my best friends for years and has helped us create these guardrails and live them out as a church. He has done an excellent job as a culture creator, so he has great credibility to write on this subject.

—Jim Putman, pastor at Real Life Ministries in Post Falls, Idaho

INTRODUCTION

One day, at a very young age, I was riding in the car with my dad on a steep mountain road that overlooked a deep valley. I don't remember the purpose of our journey, but since we're a hunting family, I am sure it had something to do with scouting a new hunting spot. Several times as we traversed this narrow mountain road, I looked over the sharp edge and saw the bottom of the valley far below. Nothing kept us from rolling to our impending doom except my dad's driving skills. As I watched him cautiously navigate the curves, he explained that some roads have guardrails along the perilous stretches to clearly mark the safe boundaries and keep vehicles from unintentionally straying into dangerous areas.

It's been a long time since that day when I learned the importance of guardrails on the road. Along the pathways of life, I also learned about the importance of the *guardrails of ministry*. I responded to God's call to ministry seventeen years ago. Along that journey, great friends and co-laborers have often reminded me of the Lord's loving kindness as he has kept me on course. His faithfulness is something I needed along the way because ministry in Jesus' church is not for the faint of heart! Looking back even now, I see assumptions I have made in error, moments that reveal my naiveté, and days of blindness due to my selfish motives. I've had great victories, in spite of myself. God has been faithful to keeping me squarely on course.

My initial call into ministry goes back to Real Life Ministries in Post Falls, Idaho. The senior pastor there, Jim Putman, and I—along with the others on our team—watched the Lord grow our church to over eight thousand in attendance in a county of one hundred thousand people. At that size, we still had *thousands* of people in small groups and some years saw more than seven hundred people baptized. As a result, churches would ask us what we were doing to make this happen. At times, we struggled to answer their questions because we couldn't quite put our finger on what was happening. But we were certain that God was doing something incredible in our midst. We knew his Spirit was laying a foundation for us and creating a platform from which we could help other churches.

God prompted us to pause during this crazy journey and intentionally evaluate some of the key practices that helped us stay on course. Jim would say, "Sometimes we might be on the rumble strips or in the ditch, but at least we are on the right road." I can look back and see that there were temptations to veer off course or to take an offramp, but we remained on the right road.

That's what I mean by *stay the course with the help of guardrails*: We were on the journey of making disciples, and by his grace, God kept us on the track to do that. Making disciples had been our primary aim since the beginning of the church, and yet we risked unintentionally straying from the disciple making path and sometimes even faced the temptations of intentionally following a different path. We could have easily become sidetracked by the temptations associated with seeking numerical church growth, big Sunday morning "productions" that draw the crowds, or even notoriety that comes from cultivating a public image. However, pursuing these things can negatively affect our efforts to make disciples. We needed to identify what it would take to stay on course for the long haul.

As we evaluated the way we had navigated the sometimes bumpy—but always exhilarating—road of ministry, we discovered some practices that are vital to staying on the healthy road of disciple making. We identified seven essential practices, and these "seven essentials" are the guardrails that helped us to avoid making a wrong turn or go a different direction. They kept us on the right road and helped us stay the course.

I share with you these seven essential practices by way of introduction. I pray that the Holy Spirit will guide and direct you into a deeper understanding of them as you travel along your journey:

1. *Abiding in Christ*. Every step toward making true disciples must be rooted in our personal walk with the Lord.

2. *Reaching the Lost*. Many in the church believe that reaching the lost is the end goal, but with discipleship as our focus,

helping the world meet Jesus is the
beginning of the journey, not the end.

3. *Connecting the Unconnected*. Believers
   must first be connected to God in a deeper
   way, and then be connected to other
   believers in authentic relationships.

4. *Chase the Strays*. It is our responsibility
   as ministers to go after those who have
   pulled away from the body of Christ and
   to draw them close to help them grow and
   connect.

5. *Shepherd Toward Spiritual Maturity*.
   We must guide believers into a place of
   maturity in Christ, not leaving them to
   remain stagnant or struggling.

6. *Release Leaders*. Helping believers discover
   and develop their potential in Christ and
   releasing them to use their gifting for
   the kingdom of God is vital for healthy
   disciple making.

7. *Function as a Team*. The greatest tool we
   have as a church is unity.

Having established my foundation in making disciples at Real Life, God began stirring my wife, Amber, and me to step away from Real Life in 2009 and expand the kingdom of God in another location. The guardrail practices above, which will be our focus throughout this book, would be tested in new ways—ways I had never before experienced. God called our family to Houston, Texas, after much waiting, toil, and prayer, where we served at Metropolitan Baptist Church for three years. We helped them transition into a biblical, disciple making church. I knew from past experience that their—and my—spiritual health was not going to happen by accident; it requires our effort and divine guidance from God. Transitioning an older, established church required setting strong boundary markers to keep them on the road of disciple making. Without these boundaries, it's easy for anyone making this transition to say things like, "We've never done it this way," or, "Don't change my church."

During my experiences there, God clarified my beliefs about leading a disciple making church and he confirmed these seven essential practices as effective guardrails. This book contains the precious truths I have taken away from that process. Now, as a senior pastor leading another church, I recognize that God will use these seven essentials to help build an effective disciple making body. We must embrace them as protective boundaries for our ministry.

While speaking at conferences and consulting with churches, I encounter pastors and church leaders who desperately want to make disciples. They dream of leading a church that fulfills the Great Commission. But something happens, and they find themselves once again on an offramp or, even worse, heading toward a cliff that may result in serious damage to their local church.

This book is designed to challenge you not only to implement the seven essential practices in your church, but also to personally live them out. One of the greatest things the Lord has taught me about discipleship is this:

Being a disciple is not about *what I do*, but about *who I am*!

Let's explore that truth together. Come, travel the road with me. Reflect and receive the challenge to see how to put in place the guardrails God gives us. He guards us from pitfalls for our health, both in our personal walk and in our corporate journey as the church.

Take Action

Read

Prepare yourself for the next chapters by reading John 15:9-17 and learning about the importance of love and abiding in Christ.

Reflect

Ask yourself these questions as you evaluate your own spiritual life:

1. What is a pivotal moment in my life where God protected me from imminent spiritual danger?

2. What has God taught me about one of the seven guardrails listed above?

3. How has God clarified the importance of making disciples in my life?

Act

Identify one of the seven guardrails listed above that you most want to explore as you continue reading this book.

1

ABIDE IN CHRIST

If the goal of our journey is to make disciples of Jesus, we must first learn how to *abide in Christ—the first essential practice or guardrail in a disciple making church.* That is, before we can make healthy disciples, we must first *be* a healthy disciple.

This truth became clear to me one night when my wife, Amber, and I were with a group of friends who felt called to plant a church with us. While we talked about how to reach certain people groups and discussed strategies for bringing the gospel to them, one of our group members named Protus spoke up. He's a great friend of mine from Kenya and he made a powerful statement during that discussion: *"If we are not first in prayer and in close relationship with Jesus, then we have nothing to bring our neighbors."*

Oh how true that is! The church must first press into Jesus Christ. Before we can effectively minister to anyone around us, we must be in close relationship with Jesus, who will fill us with his grace and mercy as we extend grace and mercy to others.

The first protective guardrail is to *abide in Christ*. This skill is not always easy to understand, even after years in ministry. When I hear "abide in Christ," I still sometimes think of a pristine park where I am supposed to sit in some deep, meditative state. Although there is nothing wrong with a practice like this, it doesn't give us the whole picture. We can understand abiding more completely by looking at the agricultural concept of grafting branches.

Grafting branches from one grapevine to another is a common practice in developing a thriving vineyard. Winemakers use this process to cultivate healthier plants by removing a branch from a vine that is susceptible to disease, and joining it to a disease-resistant vine. They also use grafting to protect branches from insects, which may damage the root system of one vine but not the other. The grafting process produces more abundant and higher quality fruit.

Jesus gives us an incredible metaphor of a vine and branches to represent our relationship with him in John 15. Much like branches that are grafted to a vibrant vine in order to produce better grapes, we are grafted to Christ, who is our life-giving vine. A branch flourishes and produces fruit when it remains connected to a healthy vine. We too will flourish and become fruitful when we remain in close relationship with Christ, our source of spiritual health and life.

A branch cut from an unhealthy vine will not produce any fruit at all, unless it is connected to a healthy vine. Likewise, Jesus says that if we do not remain connected to him, we can do nothing (John 15:4). Andrew Murray, a nineteenth-century pastor, wrote in his book *Abide in Christ*, "The great secret of abiding in Christ is the deep conviction that we are nothing, and he is everything."

Abiding is essential for making disciples. That's our calling as the branches. In fact, it encompasses *all* we are called to do. We must spend time with Jesus in prayer, learn to love and apply his Word, and listen to the Holy Spirit who flows through us as we remain connected to Christ and his Word. When we abide in these ways, God will produce fruit in us (John 15:5).

It is not the job of the branch to produce fruit. The vine provides everything the branch needs. In another of his books, *The True Vine*, Murray assures us, "You are the branch. You need be nothing more. You need not for one single moment of the day take upon you the responsibility of the Vine. You need not leave the place of entire dependence and unbounded confidence."

Abiding in Jesus will, of course, always lead to action, but the abiding must come first. When we abide, the Holy Spirit will fill us and prompt us to act. Likewise, we must also prioritize this with the church, calling them to abide in Jesus. This is vital, because the abundant fruit Jesus produces when we remain close to him is becoming healthy disciples ourselves and then making healthy disciples of others.

I've had many discussions with various church staff members over the years, and I have often asked the question, "How do you and your team discuss your personal walk with Jesus?" The most common reply is, "We don't." I do not think it is by chance that, as leaders, many of us falter in our ability to make healthy disciples or to lead a healthy disciple making church because we do not discuss or put priority on the most important practice of all—abiding in Christ. How can we truly walk in relationship with each other and with God without sharing personal victories and struggles?

Before Jesus sends us to save a group of hurting people, he first teaches us to walk intimately with him and to be in close relationship with those on our own team. Maybe you have not established this as an intentional guardrail and you find yourself off course or in the ditch. Have you taken the different path, one called, "do things for christ," rather than, "abide in Christ"? It's time to accept the truth that the only thing you must do is stay connected to Jesus. He is responsible for all the outcomes!

Take Action

Read

Open your Bible and read John 15:5-6.

Reflect

Consider these questions for yourself, and then discuss them with your team:

1. Am I too busy *doing* for Christ rather than *abiding* in Him?

2. What does it look like for me as a leader to abide in Christ?

3. How can I encourage my leaders to abide in Christ?

4. What must we stop or start doing to build an abiding-in-Christ culture within our team?

5. How can we encourage those in our church or organization to abide in Christ?

Act

Make time in the next few days to actively meditate on Christ's words in John 15:5-6 as you draw insights and energy from him to make disciples.

★ ·

2

REACH THE LOST

My greatest fear growing up was getting lost. It terrified me so much at times that while hunting as a young boy, I considered never going into the woods again. My fear of being lost would sometimes even cause panic attacks. One particular time, when I was about ten years old, my dad and I were deer hunting, and an awful snowstorm blew in. The day was nearly over, and we had only an hour or two left of daylight. I was walking alone back to our pickup truck, far enough from my dad that I could get lost. Then, the snow became blinding. I struggled to see even a few feet in front of me. The next five minutes felt like five hours as I struggled to get my bearings. I remember feeling short of breath, fighting the panic, and trying to keep my mind focused. I was terrified of being lost in the woods during a horrible storm. By God's grace, I stumbled onto a main road and within ten minutes after that, I made it to the truck where my dad was waiting. It took years of battling that fear to conquer it, and today, I love the outdoors and the adventure of traversing God's creation.

I think back to that day and draw parallels to the world around us now. When I see so many people lost and separated from God, my heart aches for them because I know that feeling. My stomach sinks as I consider that those who are spiritually lost have no idea of the perilous state they are in. It ignites a fire in my soul that I believe motivates me in my calling in Christian ministry.

A significant part of the discipleship process is *reaching the lost*—the second guardrail. Unfortunately, what I have seen in the church today is that we alternate between two extremes. Either we establish our church structures to support a fortress mindset that appeals only to those who have made it inside the fort, or we focus solely on "getting people saved." In either case, the rest of the discipleship process is ignored or forgotten.

While I commend the courage of those who preach the gospel on a street corner or hand out literature with the path to salvation, I want to suggest a bigger and more holistic approach to our second guardrail principle, which is reaching the lost.

When Jesus walked the earth with his disciples, his method of ministry embodied the message he preached. Did you catch that? *His methods embodied the message.* His very life reflected the truth of the gospel. The message of the gospel is woven like fabric with the threads of grace, love, truth, forgiveness, and mercy. Jesus demonstrated in tangible ways each of those concepts so that the gospel became alive. The *message* of Jesus Christ was lived out in the *method* of Jesus Christ.

Jesus lived the message of the gospel by modeling it through action. We see this in the way he diffused the situation with the woman caught in adultery; how he gently, but firmly, revealed the sinful lifestyle of the woman at the well; and how he marveled at the faith of the Roman centurion and healed his servant. He was the embodiment of the message. When he told his disciples to go and preach the kingdom of God, he meant for them to not only teach the gospel with their words, but also to model the gospel in the way they lived their lives.

Stay the Course

We, as Christ followers, are called to go and make disciples of Jesus Christ. He makes this clear in the Great Commission of Matthew 28: "Therefore, go and make disciples of all nations" (vv. 19-20). This passage means that our churches must reach the lost—it's part of our calling. We must individually reach out to those who are lost and help them find their way home. Also, our church and organization structure must work in such a way that we not only reach them, but also help them connect in the church. So go out into the world and share your life with those around you. Even more so, be the message of Christ as you walk out the methods of Christ.

The idea of sharing your life in a way that can reach lost people may seem ambiguous. That's why many church leaders and pastors have asked me, "How do we do that?" I tell them, "You have to choose to go after them." That's where it starts. The church has at times adopted a "build it and they will come" mentality. Some may join a group or attend your church on their own initiative, but most will not. You have to open up your life and get in the trenches with people. Amber and I do everything we can to connect with lost people. We invite them into our home, we have neighborhood barbecues, and we invite families from our kids' sports teams to just hang out with us. We choose to go after people by opening up and sharing our lives with them. It's why I titled this principle "*reach* the lost," and not "*catch* the lost." We have to reach out, go after, and pursue the lost by sharing our lives.

Implementing this principle starts with you as a leader. Sharing our lives with the lost must define who we are. I've heard some leaders argue, "Well, I do not have the gift of evangelism." It is true that we all have different gifts, but every one of us can share our lives with the world around us and clearly communicate that we are Christ followers. I believe we have damaged the church by so strongly segregating spiritual gifts. Reaching the lost is everyone's job, not just one pastor that has a specific gift.

Staff and leaders in the church should model for volunteers in the church a lifestyle of sharing their faith and making disciples. This practice will then become part of the culture of a church. When we resist segregating evangelism to a department, our church body begins to live out this principle. It becomes a protective guardrail against thinking that only certain people are qualified to share their faith. Our staff, leaders, and volunteers can then work together to develop strategies and seek organic ways to reach anyone and everyone that is outside our walls.

Take Action

Read

Open your Bible and read Luke 19:10.

Reflect

Now ask yourself and challenge your team with these questions:

1. When was the last time I personally led someone to Christ?

2. How do I equip ministry volunteers to share their faith?

3. How is my church doing at reaching the unchurched?

4. What strategic community partnership could my church pursue to meet the needs of the lost world?

Act

Here are some practical ways to ensure you are instituting the "reach the lost" guardrail principle:

- Pray for the salvation of those you know who are separated from God. But don't stop there. Call them or take them to lunch—just care for them.

- If you are on staff or you volunteer in a church, begin to discuss and challenge those around you to share Christ with others. Go after the lost!

- Invite a friend, co-worker, or family member who does not know Jesus to just spend time with you and perhaps have a spiritual conversation with you, too.

★ ·

3

CONNECT THE UNCONNECTED

I recently noticed a sign hanging in a church foyer asking, "Are you connected?" As I stopped and read that sign, I wondered what factors determine whether or not a person is connected?

For most of my years in ministry, I have worked hard at helping people in the church connect in various ways, which is the third guardrail—*connect the unconnected*. During my time as pastor of small groups at Real Life Ministries, and now as senior pastor of Real Life Ministries Texas, I have learned that connection is a significant part of spiritual growth. Discussions I have with other church leaders about the definition of "true connection" often lead to arguments. If you spend much time around me or read my blog, you will quickly realize that I strongly believe that you *must* be connected to a local church in a meaningful way. Yet when I sat down to write this book I thought, *Wow! What do I really mean by that?* An even better question I've asked myself is *What would Jesus say about it?*

A story from the life of Christ in Luke 5 sheds some light on the answers for those questions. Peter and his buddies had been fishing all night. They were tired as they washed their nets. Jesus approached them and got into their boat. After he taught the crowds, he asked Peter to head back out and fish some more. I can just imagine Peter being tired, exhausted, frustrated, and admittedly empty-handed from their previous outing. Yet Peter gives in, and they go out toward the deep waters.

In the deep waters, Jesus performs an incredible miracle, and they pull in the haul of all hauls. They now had bragging rights for decades among the other fishermen. The boats were so full they almost sank! Jesus, the greatest teacher who ever lived, uses this moment not only to teach, but also to call these men into a relationship unlike any they had ever known.

He literally and metaphorically brought them into the deeper waters.

Connection in the church often involves a commitment that goes beyond the surface. It can include volunteering in a ministry, serving as a greeter and handing out bulletins, or even joining a small group. Each of these is important and can serve a greater purpose, but I would ask you, *What does it truly mean to be connected and to go into the deep waters?*

From Scripture, we can see that the premise for connection is *following Jesus*. We become connected to Christ and his body as we follow and obey. Jesus first calls his disciples to follow him, and then he engages them in serving others. Following comes *before* serving. Jesus began to build a relationship with his disciples before he asked them to feed a crowd, much less go out in his name preaching the gospel.

I believe the church in North America would experience a radical transformation if we would first embrace Jesus' concept of being truly connected. Jesus gave us a model in the way he pursued the disciples (Matthew 4:19-22). We must, first and foremost, help people connect on a deeper level with God and with other believers in an authentic and accountable relationship toward growth in spiritual maturity. Serving in the church would then come from a place of spiritual health and stability that can only originate from Jesus. As a result, I think burnout would decrease among church leaders and our focus on healthy disciple making communities would increase.

I often tell other pastors that I am not passionate about small groups themselves; small groups are merely a vehicle. Unfortunately, churches can make small groups the end goal. They tend to think that if we just get lots of people in groups, we are successful. This is only partially true. Jesus did not just gather the twelve disciples and say, *Great! Now that I have you all here together, the kingdom of God is complete.* Small groups are the vehicle that provides the environment for people to connect on a deeper level to God and to each other. I am passionate about what *can happen* in small group—such as connection to God and to other people—but not about the group itself.

You might be tempted to think that Sunday morning services are irrelevant to true connection in the body of Christ. So what do we do with Sunday morning service? Do we abandon it? Absolutely not! If we really understand the dynamics of connecting the unconnected as an essential part of learning to follow Jesus, then Sunday services actually grow in importance. Our large group gatherings play a bigger part than just singing, teaching, and preaching. Weekend services become a connecting field. Staff will greet people and invite them to connect with others. Likewise, ministry teams and members seek to connect those who come to the weekend services.

Connecting the unconnected is a guardrail principle for church leaders. This keeps us on the road of disciple making. Regardless of how long someone has been a Christian, every person needs to be connected. We must provide those opportunities and create healthy environments for spiritual growth. My hope is that we move the question of connection from a sign in the foyer to real connections that lead to life-changing behavior in all of our churches.

Take Action

Read

Open your Bible and read 1 Thessalonians 2:8-12.

Reflect

Now answer these questions:

1. Am I connected to Christians in an environment where I am being discipled? If not, what steps could I take to ensure I am connected on a deeper level to God and to others?

2. What would it look like for leaders in my ministry to disciple the volunteers under their care, all in the context of a relational environment?

3. How does our church help people connect?

Act

Make a plan to help your church become more intentional about connecting people to relational small groups.

4

CHASE THE STRAYS

I love watching documentaries and education-al programs about wildlife. When perusing television channels, I rarely flip past something produced by National Geographic. One of my favorite specials is about African lions.

Here's the scene: It's the classic African Serengeti landscape, heat waves rising from the earth, distorting the camera's view. Colorful birds crisscross the sky, and the camera zooms in on a herd of wildebeests. The screen shows hundreds of these animals grunting and grazing their way across the plains in search of a water-hole. The commentator describes the typical habits of the wildebeest, even though you know the show is about lions—hungry lions.

The camera pans, and you see several ears poking just above the sun-bleached grass. A number of female lions watch the nervous herd of wildebeests pass by. Their tails flick back and forth at pesky flies, yet their eyes remain fixed on the herd.

Then it happens, what you knew was inevitable. One of the wildebeests, for whatever reason—sickness, injury, or stupidity—separates from the herd, its head down, feeding on grass. I watch as the poor wildebeest strays farther and farther from the safety of the herd.

I always thought the lions should pounce at that moment, but they never do. They know what they are doing. One or two of the lions go between the wildebeest and the herd, scaring the lone wildebeest, which bolts and runs away. Often, it runs farther and farther from the safety of its friends. At that time, all protection is gone and the herd's straying friend is alone. Lions spring out from the grass, as if out of nowhere. The trap had been laid, and within seconds, the circle of life continues for some and ends for the lone wildebeest.

This picture of nature is how I have often viewed what happens in the church with those that make up her body. Jesus even refers to us using flock language, calling us sheep (John 10). Even more, he refers to Satan as a roaring lion, seeking to devour us (1 Peter 5:8).

Today in the church, I so often see people begin to stray from God and the flock for various reasons—priorities, sin, jobs, or activities. They become busy and distracted with life, and before they know it, they are separated from the herd.

The fourth guardrail practice is *chase the strays*. We know that danger lies out in the grass, yet even with God, our shepherd, we can become a spiritual meal for the Evil One. We, as Christians, have a responsibility not only to remain connected to Christ ourselves, but also to go after the strays. Too often, even pastors do not know where the sheep of their flock have gone. I believe we owe it to each other to chase after someone when we see a gap begin to grow.

As a pastor, I know that I cannot shepherd every person in my church. It is my responsibility to create a culture of chasing strays. I need to make sure it is happening, not necessarily do it all myself. The staff, small group leaders, and volunteers must know that this is a guardrail for our church. We are commanded by God to care for his sheep, and when they stray, we go after them. This guardrail principle, like the others, is about building a culture that ensures this is happening. It must become who we are—people who, like Jesus, chase those who stray.

Ezekiel 34 lists "seeking out the strays" as one of the acts of true shepherding. Leaders must model this type of shepherding for those we lead so that we create a shepherding culture. It begins as an organized activity but becomes organic and a personal value for all those we lead. As a pastor, or shepherd of people, we must know where our leaders, volunteers, and attendees are. We must ask, *Who is missing? Who is disconnecting?* We must know the answers to these questions, because God expects that from us. Neglecting this command from Ezekiel 34 can leave our people separated from the herd, making them prey for the Spiritual Predator.

So how do you chase the strays? First, you must know who is missing. Begin asking questions, looking around for those you do not see or have not seen recently. If the family who attends your group or sits in the same spot every week is missing, you have to go after them. You may want to try what I do every week: I sit down and think through whom I have not seen. Then I pursue them through phone calls, meetings, home visits, and the like. A culture of caring for and noticing those who are missing must be built up. Remember that it takes time and that it will not happen if those who are in the highest positions of shepherding do not lead by example.

Take Action

Read

Open your Bible and Read Luke 15:3-7.

Reflect

Ask yourself these questions.

1. Do I notice when people are missing from weekend services?

2. How do I know if people are missing from their relational environment (small group)?

3. What could I do to value, notice, and pursue those who are missing in our flock?

4. What changes can I make or what processes can I put into place that will ensure that our staff notices who is missing and intentionally pursues them?

Act

This week, call someone this week whom you notice is missing from small group or weekend services. Let them know you missed them. Ask how you can be praying for them and encourage them to come back.

★ . . . .

5

SHEPHERD TOWARD SPIRITUAL MATURITY

Elk are incredible animals. I have spent the better part of twenty-five years watching, studying, and hunting them. In my opinion, they are one of God's most magnificent creations. Every year as I see these large, powerful animals, God teaches me something new about himself, his creation, or even myself.

The fifth guardrail principle for a disciple making church is to *shepherd people toward spiritual maturity*. Believe it or not, while I was bow hunting one time, a female elk taught me a tremendous lesson about shepherding people.

I was pressing through some of the most awful brush that the North Idaho forest has to offer. I was climbing, groaning, and whining out loud as I made my way through the dense trees and bushes. I stumbled across a huge herd of elk that had been using the thick brush for cover. Instantly, the herd I approached bolted in every direction. I hadn't seen them leave, but branches shook and snapped all around me as the herd scattered, letting me know they were gone. My prey had left. So instinctively, I stopped and put my elk call in my mouth and began to call out as if I were a lost elk calf. I was essentially pleading for the herd to come back and save me. I was hoping they would come close enough for me to take a shot with my bow. To my surprise, a huge female elk came running toward me. She called to me and circled the area around me, trying to locate me, convinced that I was a poor little calf lost in the brush. She knew it was important to keep calves close to the herd. She stomped her hoof, trying to ward off predators, and beckoned me to follow her. It's like she couldn't tell I was a human! It was not until I literally waved my arms at her that she gave up and ran back to the herd.

I learned something about shepherding in the church from my encounter with that female elk. Jesus is the great shepherd, and in Scripture we are taught that every believer should shepherd others toward spiritual maturity. In the church, we are to look through a lens that causes us to see people with the same care and concern that Jesus does. The elk provides a great analogy for us: Because the female elk was concerned for the calf's health and safety, she shifted her focus to intentionally seek out and encourage it. Likewise, we must understand that the spiritual health and safety of those around us should be our concern. We are commanded in Scripture to encourage each other daily (Hebrews 3:12-14).

To effectively and daily encourage others and press them toward Christ, we must be in proximity to them. Sadly, in church today we have put so much emphasis on what happens on Sunday morning that we have followed the culture into a world of loneliness. We have not learned the importance of keeping people close, much like the female elk sought to keep her calf close in my story. We have left people to fend for themselves while believing we are succeeding because we can produce an entertaining Sunday morning. Sundays are vital, but they can never take the place of the proximity needed to shepherd someone toward maturity.

Unfortunately, we sometimes view maturity in Christ as having a strong education or thorough Bible knowledge. Bible knowledge is important, and I encourage you to train your staff, leaders, and church members in solid doctrinal principles. But just because someone knows the facts doesn't mean they apply them to their life. That's why becoming mature takes shepherding.

Discipleship is a process where we follow the Holy Spirit's leading as we help each other to be more like Christ. We take knowledge from Scripture and live it out in real life, learning to love others as Jesus loves us and care for others as he cares for us.

Whether you are a pastor, an elder, or a small group leader, if you follow Christ, you are called to help people grow in spiritual maturity. Without this guardrail in the church we can never remain on track toward leading people to spiritual growth. Without it, we forget what it means for the church to win. Winning is making disciples, and disciple making cannot happen if we do not intentionally shepherd people into spiritual maturity.

Take Action

Read

Open your Bible and read John 21:15-18.

Reflect

Ask yourself these questions:

1. Who am I discipling toward spiritual maturity? How am I leading that person to spiritual maturity?

2. What am I doing to intentionally disciple my team?

3. What changes can I make to help create a shepherding culture in our church?

Act

Identify one individual whom you can begin to intentionally shepherd.

6

EQUIP AND RELEASE LEADERS

I love March Madness—the time of year when sixty-four college basketball teams have the opportunity to make a run for the National Collegiate Athletic Association (NCAA) title. The stories, players, and coaches that emerge are incredible. I can remember watching many of the famous matchups and unbelievable buzzer beaters over my thirty years of following this tournament.

There are very few coaches on the planet I respect more than Mike Krzyzewski, or "Coach K" as he's called, the coach of Duke University's basketball team. His leadership on the floor and his knowledge of the game are incredible, yet what I respect most about him is something very few notice: Coach K is an amazing disciple maker in the game of basketball. The results of his efforts are evident to all by the types of players he turns out. For example, six of Coach K's former players are now NCAA college basketball coaches themselves. Talk about equipping and releasing leaders! What a great testimony to his skills as a coach that his former players went on to do just what he did as they invest in the lives of other young men.

The sixth guardrail principle is equipping and releasing leaders. Of all the essential practices of a disciple making church, this one is dearest to my heart. A key component in developing people is releasing them to be who God made them to be. Like Coach K, I love to give people the opportunity to get in the game and to learn how to become great players, too.

Once they begin to take on responsibility, they can learn and eventually become great coaches, or developers, of people themselves. In my opinion, there is no greater reward than to see the kingdom expand as the people I've invested in begin to develop others who, in turn, go and influence others for Jesus Christ.

Jesus modeled this principle for us and we see the early church carry it on as Christianity grew. Jesus gave his disciples the opportunity to be involved in his ministry, even while he was on earth. They got off the bench and jumped into the game. Whether Jesus let them minister to the crowds or sent them out to preach the good news of the kingdom, he let them play in the game. Often in the church, people are told to sit, spectate, and watch the pastors perform. Not so with Jesus. He developed disciples who knew how to go and make disciples. He let them play so that one day, they themselves would be great coaches of other players, too.

If we in the church lead someone to Christ who begins attending services, we usually view it as a win. That's great, of course, but true success, as defined in the Bible, is *making a disciple who can make a disciple*. I would contend that we have not truly succeeded until those we have either led to Christ or discipled are making disciples on their own. It must move beyond us! In Scripture, we see this principle in the life of Peter.

Christ calls Peter to follow him and spends three years building a relationship with him and discipling him. We then have the privilege of seeing Peter make disciples in the Book of Acts (e.g., Acts 2:14-36, 3:11-26, 4:8-13), and later in the epistles authored by him (1 Peter and 2 Peter).

Those players who Coach K developed are now out developing other players, who may themselves become coaches one day. The church must develop, raise up, and release leaders. The church today seems to operate with a fear that if we let people go, everything will fall apart. I see few leaders who easily trust the Holy Spirit for this, but in Christ, it can be a regular part of the process!

I know this from experience. When I was small groups pastor at Real Life Ministries in Post Falls, we released people to go make disciples faster than we could count. Organizationally it created problems, for sure, but our people's ownership of making disciples soared. We freed them up to make disciples—just as Jesus freed people to do as he did. Too often, I work with leaders who are building church systems that force volunteers to be dependent on the staff. The church becomes built around the staff or the senior pastor, rather than around Jesus and his commission to go make disciples. Disciple making churches must be willing to let people go!

I think about this principle all the time with my own kids, as well as with those who are in my church. I ask myself if I am developing them to not just be disciples, but also to go out into the world and *make disciples*. I want each of my kids to know exactly how to make a disciple. I want a church filled with people who understand exactly how to make disciples of Jesus. That way they are not dependent on me! They can become spiritual coaches who develop other players, even other coaches. When we understand this principle of releasing disciples to make disciples and commit to it, we develop stronger families and more effective churches.

I want to offer a few key takeaways about this important principle of releasing your people: It is important to make the distinction between those who lead in the church, either by gifting or position, and those who are disciples of Jesus. Every believer in the church should be in discipling relationships—being discipled and learning to disciple others. Every believer in the church is called to be a minister and a servant (2 Corinthians 5:18). However, not everyone has the gift of leadership. As you disciple all types of people, leaders will emerge. Once you identify a leader, develop and release them when they are ready. Leaders in the church are called to be disciples who make disciples and also to shepherd the body of Christ and coach those who will lead alongside and after them.

When we build this guardrail and people are being raised up and released, our churches become filled with people who raise up others like Coach K did. The result is a legacy in the kingdom of God, a kingdom that never ends, a kingdom we can participate in here and now.

Take Action

Read

Open your Bible and read Ephesians 4:11-16.

Reflect

Consider these questions:

1. How can I release more responsibility to others on my team?

2. What process do I have in place to know if my team is raising up the next generation of leaders?

3. What apprenticeship system do we have in our small groups?

Act

A key part of discipleship is giving people places to play. Identify one new place in your area of ministry where someone could volunteer.

7

FUNCTION AS
A TEAM

Have you ever played a game of tug-o-war? Several years ago while I served on staff at Real Life Ministries, we had an incredible event during which an epic tug-o-war took place. Let me set the stage for you. The event was called "Battle on the Bluff." It was an all-day event where men from all our small groups gathered to spend the day competing, eating, and enjoying an incredible northern Idaho summer day. A man in our church owned a great piece of property overlooking the beautiful Lake Coeur d'Alene. The field of play was a huge park-like field interspersed with evergreen trees.

We had massive amounts of all kinds of barbecued meat. (That, of course, is the primary checklist item for any successful men's event.) Along with great food, we had all kinds of games, ranging from horseshoes to archery target competitions. Throughout the day's events, we would pass by this huge tug-o-war pit. It was going to be the climactic event of the day. We were divided into teams based on the region where we lived to compete for being the manliest men in northern Idaho. The smack talk started early in the day, and tension rose with the temperature as the day progressed.

One team had most of the largest guys, who outweighed most of the other participants by at least two hundred pounds. That was not *our group*; they were our competition. So I put my brain and sports know-how to work. My group of guys was the smallest, but we had some solid athletes among us. We huddled up and developed a strategy.

"It's all about unity, guys," I told them. I knew if we worked in unison, we could win.

We began the contest. Soon, two teams emerged on top as they mowed through the competition to the final round—my team and the heavyweights. The final battle came down to our two groups. One team would be taking a huge mud bath.

I rallied my guys again. By this point, we had perfected our strategy. I called out our cadence of unity, *1 – 2 – 3 – pull, 1 – 2 – 3 – pull, 1 – 2 – 3 – pull.* Like a well-oiled machine, we dragged those big boys into the mud, despite their massive weight and strength advantage. It was our strategy that kept us together, creating a powerfully united team. When we pulled, we all pulled together, and when we rested, we all rested together. Our coordinated, consistent effort as a team helped us accomplish our goal.

The same strategy works in the church. God calls us to work together in unity so that we will be able to defeat the evil forces around us. He tells us that when we do, nothing can stand against us. In fact, Jesus' prayer in John 17 says that when we are unified, the world around us will be drawn to him.

Did you know that our greatest evangelistic tool is unity? Our seventh and final guardrail principle for being a disciple making church is to *function as a team.* The greatest way to reach our communities is to be unified as we love and care for those in our church body. So often we think our first step toward evangelistic outreach is to produce a big event in our community, yet we forget that we must first be unified within our churches. It's no wonder the church today struggles to reach a lost world when we are so internally disjointed. We must function as a unified team in order to be effective at making disciples. We must fight for relationships and work together toward a common goal, or it will only be a matter of time before we find ourselves knee-deep in mud, losing our spiritual tug-o-war against the Enemy of our souls.

Looking back on my time at Real Life, senior pastor Jim Putman taught me such important lessons about leadership and frankly, biblical relationships. He always said that it's a fight: "We have to fight for unity and remain together." During those days, I did not always feel like being unified with my team! If it wasn't my personal feelings being hurt, it was some other issue threatening to drive us apart. Yet we remained committed to the cause of Christ and committed to each other. How can we ever hope to have true biblical success in the church if we are not walking in unity? How can we ever expect God to bless what we are doing if we are not in relational or organizational unity with those closest to us?

Jesus tells us to love our neighbor. That does not just mean the person living in the box next to us. He really means those closest to us. Regrettably, many churches want to reach the world and have "decisions for Christ," yet do not decide to fight for the relationships with other co-laborers on a church staff or in church leadership.

You will recall that our first guardrail is about abiding in Christ. Jim often says, "If the church is the body of Christ, then part of abiding in Christ is relationship within the body of Christ." Functioning as a team means that we abide in the relationships closest to us. We must fight for and be in relationship with each other if we are to accomplish anything significant for the kingdom of Christ.

So how do we do that? We must choose to put relationships first. We must view those we work with as God's children and not as barriers or people "we have to put up with" to accomplish our work in ministry. We have to lay down our pride to put others before us. I would encourage you to find ways to get to know and minister to those with whom you serve, regardless of the distance between you and them on your "org chart." Find ways to build relational unity so that your journey together is a joy, not just a task you accomplish as a team.

Take Action

Read

Open your Bible and read John 17.

Reflect

Ask yourself these questions.

1. What relational rifts with my team member do I need to reconcile?

2. How can I support and encourage someone in another ministry area of my church this week?

3. How do my relationships with my team members demonstrate the love of Christ to the unsaved people around us?

Act

Pay close attention to Jesus' prayer of unity for you and for me. Seek a closer relationship with someone on your team this week by spending intentional time with him or her.

★. . . . .

CONCLUSION

To close out this book and tie together the seven practices, let me tell you about the importance of paying attention to the details. I was reminded of how important this is several years ago when I took a guy (I will call "Joe") elk hunting with me. Another friend asked me as a favor to take him hunting. I called Joe before the trip, and we agreed on a place to meet and the location where we would hunt, just like normal. (I learned some great life lessons later from the assumptions I had made about Joe by this point.)

Joe and I met at 3:30 a.m. at a nearby gas station and we set out to hunt elk. We chit-chatted on the way, and he told me of his previous hunting exploits. He used words and phrases that raised some red flags for an experienced hunter like me. I was beginning to think that he had no idea how to hunt, but there was no turning back now.

When we arrived and began to unload, I noticed that several things were wrong with his gear. Especially concerning was his bowstring, which was very frayed, and his quiver, which looked broken and in poor condition. I also noticed the cheap tennis shoes he was wearing. This alarmed me because I knew the chance of rain was high that day, and North Idaho Mountains, plus rain, plus hiking, plus cheap tennis shoes *equals a bad day*!

Within a few hours, elk had come around us, and Joe had a perfect chance for a shot. I called the elk in close, but he was unprepared. When he finally drew his bow, a portion of his string broke, causing his equipment as a whole to fail. As a result, the elk ran and my blood pressure went high enough to cause me a stroke. Joe's poor attention to some *important details*, his lack of preparation, and his improper care for gear led to what can only be described as an epic hunting fail. I made a mental note to do everything in my power to avoid any hunt like this in the future.

Conclusion

Our day only got worse from there. The rain began to pour, and we had to hike a mile in mud. Joe slipped and fell more times than I could count! In the process of falling several times, he finished off his half-broken quiver, breaking it completely into pieces. I bet the pieces of it are still on that hillside today!

Details of the hunt matter, even small details like the condition of your bowstring or the soundness of your quiver. In the same way, paying attention to the details of the guardrail practices can keep us on the road of disciple making. Unless we are intentional about putting them in place, we can find ourselves drifting quickly off the road. As Christians, disciple making must be a way of life. It must be intentional and always in the forefront of our minds.

Mastering hunting or any skill in life requires continued focus on the little things and doing what it takes to be successful. Ask any golfer, parent, preacher, teacher, mechanic, engineer, or entrepreneur what it takes to be successful. For all these pursuits, we have to do the appropriate little things that will, we hope, lead to success one day.

In your walk with Christ, whether you are the lead pastor, an elder, or a lay leader, you are called to be a disciple maker. We live in a world that is full of distractions. The church itself often holds on to older ways of doing things or sets up new structures of doing things—both of which can keep us from the very calling we have been given—to make disciples of Jesus. It's easy to drift or to get on the wrong road. So remember that it takes intentionality and effort.

I frequently remind the guys on my leadership team that discipleship is a grind. It's hard work, it's often messy, and it requires time, priority, and attention to the details. Even though it's difficult, we don't give up. We keep on the narrow path of discipleship, because that's what Jesus commanded us to do.

My challenge to those reading this book is that you to begin putting in place these guardrail practices in your church and in your personal life. They are for your protection, to keep you on the right road. Commit to them, and I know from experience that your focus will begin to shift toward the right measurement of success— growing disciples who know how to disciple others! My prayer for you is that you find your God-given road and that you stay the course.

BIBLIOGRAPHICAL NOTE

The quotes from Andrew Murray in Chapter 1 come from his books *Abide in Christ* and *The True Vine*, which were published in New Kensington, Pennsylvania by Whitaker House in 2002.

Brandon Guindon is lead pastor at Real Life Ministries Texas. He has a Master of Arts degree in church leadership and New Testament theology from Hope International University. Ordained at Real Life Ministries in Post Falls, Idaho, Brandon is coauthor of *Real-Life Discipleship Training Manual* and chairman of the Relational Discipleship Network Board of Directors. You can learn more about the Relational Discipleship Network at *RelationalDiscipleshipNetwork.com.*

Twitter: @BrandonGuindon

Facebook: https://www.facebook.com/BrandonGuindonAuthor